101 SILLY MONSTER JOKES

by Jovial Bob Stine

Illustrated by B.K. Taylor

SCHOLASTIC INC.
New York Toronto London Auckland Sydney

To Matty

ISBN 0-590-33889-7

23 22 21 20 -   4 5 6 7/9

Printed in the U.S.A.   01

THESE JOKES ARE A *HOWL!*

What is the Abominable Snowman's favorite food?

Cold cuts!

What sound do two vampires make when they kiss?

Ouch!

How does a monster count to 345?

On his fingers!

3

What do you get when King Kong walks through your vegetable garden?

Squash!

Why did the monster cross the road?

To bite someone on the other side!

What's the best way to call King Kong?

Long Distance!

Why did the invisible monster look in the mirror?

He wanted to make sure he still wasn't there!

Why shouldn't you invite werewolves into your house?

They shed on the couch!

What do you call a vampire that rides first class in an airplane?

A passenger!

Who has the most dangerous job in Transylvania?

Dracula's dentist!

What is more invisible than the
Invisible Man?

His shadow!

How would you describe Frankenstein's
birth?

Shocking!

Which side of King Kong has the
most fur?

The outside!

Why did the monster eat Cleveland, skip over Akron, and then eat Pittsburgh?

He didn't want to eat between meals!

What do you call it when twenty monsters begin punching, howling, biting, and tearing each other's heads off?

Party time!

Why did the doctor tell the zombie to get plenty of bed rest?

He was dead on his feet!

What do you call a vampire who bites
people when they're not looking?

Shy!

Why did Frankenstein stick his finger
in the electrical socket?

He wanted to keep up on current events!

What time is it when Godzilla sits on your watch?

Time to get a new watch!

THESE JOKES MIGHT MAKE YOU CROSS....

What would you get if you crossed a werewolf and a snowball?

Frostbite!

What would you get if you crossed a vampire with a 24-hour clock?

An all-day sucker!

What would you get if you crossed
Count Dracula with a computer?

Love at first byte!

What would you get if you crossed a
vampire with a wool scarf?

A pain in the neck!

What would you get if you crossed
Dracula and 200 candy bars?

A vampire with fang decay!

What would you get if you crossed a
watchdog with a werewolf?

A very nervous mailman!

What would you get if you crossed a
mummy with a necktie?

*A Christmas present for Dad that's
already wrapped!*

18

What would you get if you crossed a monster and a cat?

A neighborhood without any dogs!

SOME FAVORITES....

What's a monster's favorite song?

"Ghouls Just Wanna Have Fun"

What's the vampire's favorite holiday?

Fangsgiving!

Who's a monster's favorite
movie star?

Scarey Grant!

What's a monster's favorite skyscraper?

The Vampire State Building!

What is Count Dracula's favorite sport?

Skin diving!

Who's a monster's favorite comedian?

Blob Hope!

What's a monster's favorite food?

Ham and legs!

Why is baseball a monster's
favorite sport?

They like double-headers!

Where's a monster's favorite place
to swim?

Lake Eerie!

What's a monster's favorite movie?

Scar Wars

What's a monster's favorite game?

Hide and Shriek!

What's Godzilla's favorite sport?

Squash!

MORE JOKES TO HOWL OVER!

Why does Count Dracula consider himself an artist?

He likes to draw blood!

Why do mummies make good spies?

They know how to keep things under wraps!

What is normal eyesight for a monster?

20-20-20-20!

First Werewolf: Guess what? A family of humans moved into our neighborhood.

Second Werewolf: Good! Why don't you invite them over for a quick bite!

Sam: Is it true that a monster won't hurt you if you carry a flashlight?

Pam: That depends on how fast you carry it!

At Monster School, what do they call a monster who sets fire to the desks, squashes all the textbooks, and eats the exams?

Teacher's pet!

31

How do you make a monster stew?

Keep it waiting around for two or three hours!

How do you say "vampire" in Spanish?

Vampire in Spanish.

Why did the two cyclopes get into a fight?

They couldn't see eye-to-eye!

First Werewolf: How was your party
last night?
Second Werewolf: It was a howling
success!

First Monster: You don't have a brain in
your head.
Second Monster: Which head?

Clerk on Phone: Hello. City Morgue.
Count Dracula: Do you deliver?

What kind of a raincoat does Franken-stein wear on a rainy day?

A wet one!

First Invisible Man: Did you miss me when I was gone?
Second Invisible Man: Were you gone?

First Monster: What lovely eyes you have.
Second Monster: Thank you. They were a birthday present!

What do English sea monsters have
for dinner?

Fish and ships!

How can you tell if there's a monster in your sandwich?

It's too heavy to lift!

JOKES YOU CAN SINK YOUR TEETH INTO!

Why did it take the monster three hours to finish a 20-page book?

He wasn't very hungry!

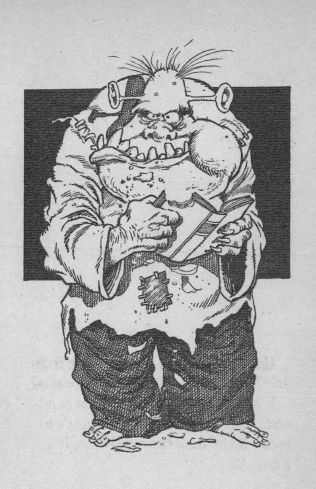

What did the monster say after he ate
Cleveland?

"What's for dinner?"

How can you tell if a monster from
another planet is a male or a female?
It's easy. Give the monster a sandwich. If he eats the sandwich, it's a
male. If she eats the sandwich, it's
a female!

A monster woke up at midnight in a terrible temper. "Where's my supper?" he yelled. "Where are the gwepel cakes? Where's my glardl soup? Where's my klagzok with meatballs?"

"Now, take it easy," his wife replied. "Can't you see I only have six hands?"

What is the difference between a monster and peanut butter?

A monster doesn't stick to the roof of your mouth!

A monster was having dinner in a restaurant and ordered soup. When the waiter brought the soup, it had a fly in it.

The monster looked into the bowl, frowned, and said, "Hey, waiter — could you remove the broth from around this fly?"

Young Monster: Hey, Ma, may I eat
New York City?
Mother Monster: Not unless you wash
your hands first!

Sam: Did you hear about the three
monsters who were arrested for
throwing a party?
Pam: Why?
Sam: They threw it across the Grand
Canyon!

First Monster: I'm starving.
Second Monster: Dinner is in
the oven.
First Monster: Oh good! Who are we
having tonight?

Clerk: Would you like this new television set delivered to your home, Mr. Godzilla?
Godzilla: No, thanks. I'll eat it here!

A monster was having dinner in a restaurant. When he finished, the waitress asked, "Did you enjoy the Blue Plate Special?"

"It was okay," said the monster. "But the pink cup and saucer had a lot more flavor!"

NEVER MIND. . . .

Did you hear the story of the vampire's sharp teeth?

Never mind — you wouldn't get the point!

Did you hear the mystery of the 5,000-year-old mummy?

Never mind — you couldn't unravel it!

Did you hear the joke about the
500-foot monster?

Never mind — it's over your head!

Did you hear the story of the monster
who ate Cleveland?

Never mind — you'd never swallow it!

Did you hear the story of the zombie's
grave?

Never mind — you wouldn't dig it.

Did you hear the story of how King Kong came down from the Empire State Building?

Never mind — you'd never fall for it!

Did you hear the joke about the Abominable Snowman?

Never mind — it would probably leave you cold!

MORE SCREAMS!

What happens to a mummy when it falls into the Nile River?

It gets wet!

What goes, "Ha-ha-ha, plop-plop-plop."?

A monster laughing its heads off!

What kind of fur do you get from a werewolf?

As fur away as you can get!

Where was Count Dracula when the lights went out?

In the dark!

What kind of beans does Godzilla like to eat?

Human beans!

Two kids were standing in front of a mummy case in a museum. A sign on the case said: 1275 B.C.

"What do you think that number means?" the first kid asked.

The second kid thought for a while. "Maybe it's the license plate number of the car that hit him!"

1275 B.C.

Mother Monster: Son, I thought I told you to drink your medicine after your bath.

Young Monster: I'm sorry, Ma. But after I finished drinking the bath, I didn't have room for the medicine!

Young Monster: Ma, I hate my teacher!
Mother Monster: Then just eat your
salad.

First Monster: Have an accident?
Second Monster: No thanks, I just had
one.

Mother Monster: Do you think we should take Junior to the zoo?

Father Monster: Certainly not! If the zoo wants him, they can come and get him!

First Monster: We must be getting close to a city.

Second Monster: Why do you say that?

First Monster: We're stepping on more people!

MONSTER KNOCK KNOCKS

Knock knock.
Who's there?
Bat.
Bat who?
Bat you can't wait to read more of these
jokes!

Knock knock.
Who's there?
Ivan.
Ivan who?
Ivan awful headache ever since God-
zilla stepped on me!

63

Knock knock.
Who's there?
Howl.
Howl who?
Howl we know *you're* not a werewolf?

Knock knock.
Who's there?
Bloody.
Bloody who?
Bloody, can you spare a dime?

Knock knock.
Who's there?
Juan.
Juan who?
Juan more monster knock
knock, please!

Knock knock.
Who's there?
Hank.
Hank who?
Hank you for your contribution to
Dracula's blood bank!

Knock knock.
Who's there?
Phil.
Phil who?
Phil my face — is it getting furry?

Knock knock.
Who's there?
Hairy.
Hairy who?
Hairy up and finish these ridiculous jokes!!

A MONSTER LANDED ON EARTH AND. . . .

A monster landed on Earth and the first thing he saw was a chicken. "Can you tell me how to get to Carnegie Hall?" the monster asked.

"Pluck, pluck," said the chicken.

"No, I don't play harp," said the monster. "I'm a bassoonist!"

A monster landed on Earth and the first thing he saw was a farmer milking a cow. "No wonder you're not getting any music," cried the monster. "Your bagpipes are filled with milk!"

A monster landed on Earth and the first thing he saw was a robin pulling a long earthworm out of the ground.

"Use a napkin," cried the monster, "or you'll get that spaghetti all over your vest!"

A monster landed on Earth and decided to take a cruise on an ocean liner. At supper time, he took a seat in the dining room.

"Would you like a menu, sir?" asked the steward.

"That won't be necessary," said the monster. "Just bring me the passenger list!"

A monster landed on Earth and the first thing he saw was a sparrow. "Can you direct me to a hotel?" he asked.

"Cheep, cheep," said the sparrow.

"It better be," the monster said. "Getting here cost me a fortune!"

CREATURE FEATURES. . . .

Did you enjoy the movie, Mr. Wolf Man?

Yes. I thought it was a howl!

Did you enjoy the movie, Mr. Mummy?

Some parts were a bit dry, but I was totally wrapped up in it!

Did you enjoy the movie, Count Dracula?

It was draining. I like films in a lighter vein!

Did you enjoy the movie, Frankenstein?

It was electrifying. It had me bolted to my seat. I found it staggering!

Did you enjoy the movie, Mr. Invisible Man?

No, I didn't like the plot. I could see right through it!

Did you enjoy the movie, Mr. Zombie?

Some parts were dead. But it staggered to life in the end.

Did you enjoy the movie, Godzilla?

I don't know. I stepped on the theater before it started!

LAST CHANCE FOR MONSTER LAUGHTER....

Why did Dr. Frankenstein put a rubber band in his monster's brain?

He wanted it to make snap decisions!

How do you make a strawberry shake?

Take it to a monster movie!

What do you get when King Kong
sneezes?

Out of the way!

What does a boy monster call a girl monster who has two heads, four yellow, drippy eyes, three nostrils, and fur growing on her neck?

Cute!

How many teeth does a vampire have?

Who knows? Do YOU want to be the one to count them?!!

What did the police do when the
monster took the freeway to town?

They made him put it back!

What are two things Frankenstein
can't have for breakfast?

Lunch and dinner!

Girl Monster: There are only four things that keep you from being a good dancer.

Boy Monster: What are they?

Girl Monster: Your feet!

First Monster: Madam, your son is gruesome, gross, and disgusting!

Mother Monster: Thank the man for all the nice compliments, Junior!

Young Monster: Ma, is it all right to eat potatoes with your fingers?

Mother Monster: No, eat the potatoes first. *Then* eat your fingers!

Sam: What do you call a person who sticks his right arm down a monster's throat?

Pam: Lefty.

Mother Monster: Stop kicking the doctor.

Young Monster: Why, Ma?

Mother Monster: You have your new shoes on!

Nurse: Doctor, there's an invisible monster in the waiting room.

Doctor: Tell him I can't see him!

Why wasn't the 500-pound monster allowed to fight in the monster boxing tournament?

There were no other lightweights in the tournament!

What is 40 feet tall, weighs two tons, steps on entire cities, and prevents forest fires?

Smokey the monster!

Young Monster: Look, Ma, I'm chasing a big man around a tree.

Mother Monster: Junior, how many times must I tell you not to play with your food!

What do you call a clean, good-looking, well-behaved monster?

A failure!